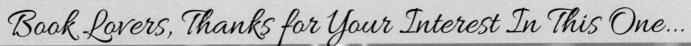

Book Lovers, Thanks for Your Interest In This One...

A Huge Shout out to my wonderful Husband Farley Williams, Daughter Danielle McDuffy (Dejhan Means) Dior, Dion & Dejhan Jr., step-children Jasmine and Keith.

To my siblings, we"ve learned a lot of our valuable life lessons together.. THANK YOU brothers, Victor and Leonard, and sisters, Ronda, Andrena and Yaminah.

ON THE SHOULDERS OF GIANTS is dedicated especially to my mom, the late Jerelene McDuffy- Hiltonen. She had big plans for me at a very early age., Oh how I wished that she was here in person to see them manifest, I finally get to see what she was talking about. LOVE YOU MOM and I Thank GOD for this journey.

On The Shoulders of Giants

All Volumes

V1, Lessons & Blessings

V2, Youth Edition

V3, All Inspirational

ENJOY YOUR READ!

Dr. Delece Williams, Author

Preface

Have you ever heard of the saying, "**STANDING IN SOMEONE ELSE'S SHOES**," as a point of reference to learning a lesson? Well, what happens when the shoes doesn't fit? In this book, we'll show you how to **"STAND ON THE SHOULDERS OF GIANTS,"** as a stepping stone to victorious living.

This book's goal is to build on multi-generational relationships with inspirational wisdom quotes for best use through the eyes of historical people. Updated experiences will also be shared as the author, *Dr. Delece Williams* showcases her montage of over *100 Celebrity* **photo moments** demonstrating how using words of wisdom can help you reach higher heights too. Dr. Delece deems it important to show you how she navigated her way to discovering maximum potential while gleaning from the star's various levels of success along with listening to some of their wisdom points.

All Original Photos are of Delece with

Keanu Reeves

Yulonda Adams

Chat Daddy

Tyler Perry

Tye Tribbett

Iyanla Vanzant

Katherine Jackson

TEACHABLE MOMENTS, DISCLOSURE AND GOAL

Each page highlights a teachable moment from a short quote spoken by well-known figures from ancient times to present day, and some wisdom points from the bible and more. The goal is to show how smart, sensitive men and women through-out history have agreed on certain basic approaches to life although they have expressed their ideas in different ways.

Each quote is taken from the **Book of Positive Quotations, Compiled and Arranged by John Cook.**

Other verbiage on each page is compiled with *Dr. Delece 's original photos that shows her engagement with celebrities as she highlights their great significance.* The hope is to inspire your greatest potential and breakthroughs for your life's positive outcomes too. **"On The Shoulders of Giants,"** *Vol. 2 (Youth Edition) and Vol. 3 (Inspirational) is available also....Enjoy!*

www.drdelece.com | drdelece@hotmail.com

Table of Content

Introduction—Youth, Elder Engagement & More

I heard this millennial say, "Why don't successful older people tell us their secrets to success and who's really helping to remove obstacles out of our way, so that we can produce best life choices too?" Meanwhile, "**_RESPECT_**" is what a lot of elders feel that's missing from some young people which is why we have such a inter-generational breakdown between the two. Upon surveying the matter, this book was birthed as a tool to help mediate between generations; *to enhance effective ways for dealing with today's youth and to help humble them enough to want to listen.* Lots of elders have the **_WISDOM they need_**," thus furthering the need to stop taking some elders for granted. *A lot of times, this matter boils down to communication, some prayer, what we value and the way we are viewing things.*

First of all, some of us adults must understand how to engage the technical appetites of young people, so that we can infuse our traditional values, especially since our words are not as popular as the virtual world (**_Facebook, Tik Tok, You tube, Google, Instagram and others_**). It was also told to me that one perfect pitch for grabbing anyone's attention is to use photos, emoji's, and to share less intimidating valuable words as possible but, get **straight to wisdom talking points.**

This book series will cover: **_Generational Communication Barriers_**, along with; *_The Inner Me Struggle_** *_Capacity Or Ability To Understand_** *_Dispensation Of Time_** and *_Hindsight is 20/20._** *Elders want to bless you with the gift of wisdom but are you listening? Elders, are you also listening to the younger generation carefully.* The ultimate goal is to help pass down **generational blessings** through quotes and my personal experiences. Come along as I share my journey of searching for success and how words of wisdom unlocked pathways for accomplishing many of my personal and professional goals in hopes of inspiring you to reach your fullest potential too.

I WORKED WITH ONE OF THE MOST INFLUENTIAL STAND-UP COMEDIANS OF ALL TIME!

DELECE & RICHARD

I wouldn't have had a chance to be in a movie with the famous **_Richard Pryor,_** if I wasn't listening to someone wise. My friend saw something in me that I didn't see in myself. Working on the **JoJo Dancer movie** was an awesome experience, Richard picked me to play a waitress. This was also when I was two months pregnant and didn't know, so I had to put my career on hold to have a baby. This was the one time when you hear people tell you that you can get pregnant if you have sex, they were right, I should have listened, but I don't regret having my beautiful daughter, just wished I would have waited in that time of my life.

CHAPTER 1—SO YOU WANNA BE A STAR!

Here's The First Quote Towards Your Journey for Success. In fact, Every Page Drops Nuggets of Wisdom In Living Color.

Keep away from people who try to belittle your ambitions. Small people always do that, but the really GREAT make you feel that you, too, can become GREAT.

-By Mark Twain

OPRAH WINFREY

Women of Brewster's Place

One year before working with Richard, I never thought I'd meet this beautiful woman right here, <u>Oprah Winfrey</u>. *She ranks as the most influential woman in the world that started in media.* During my high school years, Oprah was my life-line because I was the only black girl in the entire town which meant that there were not a lot of black women images on television where I lived. When her daily shows came on, I had begun to appreciate my black skin along with receiving confidence in knowing that I too can be great some day.

My dream has now become true. One year, I was able to work side by side with Oprah on the tv show called **Women of Brewster's Place** for four months as a stand-in. This opportunity also allowed me to work on other Oprah projects, like **"There Are No Children Here"** and more. In this moment in time, I stood in her shadow and it changed my entire life while being in aw of her wisdom.

> **I was raised to sense what someone wanted me to be and be that kind of person. It took me a long time not to judge myself through someone else's eyes.**
> **-By Sally Fields**

This photo was taken on the set of **"Women of Brewster's Place,"** as you can see from the props of an old magazine and more.

It was fun to see how they re-created a room from back in the day. I loved working with _**Oprah Winfrey**_.

ALEX HALEY

> **You have to deal with the fact that your life is your life.**
> **-By Alex Haley**

Many celebrities would visit Oprah's studio while we were filming. I will never forget meeting _**Mr. Alex Haley,**_ _the American writer and the author of the 1976 book, called ROOTS. The Saga of an American Family that aired in 1977 to a record-breaking audience of 130 million viewers._ This was a phenomenal time because he had just wrapped up filming and in this moment, I remember him telling us about his new movie project called **"QUEEN,"** starring _Halle Berry_. I also got a chance to work with her as well, stay tuned for more details.

Wil Gatlin and I are still friends until this day. At the time, he worked as a caterer on vending trucks and they fed us very well. This photo was taken in the Hyde Park community of Chicago with Actress **_Irma P. Hall_**. *She is an American actress who appeared in many films and television shows from the 1970's. She was also the Big Ma character in the original Soul Food movie.* Upon showing up for my daily work schedule, I got a chance to sit around most of the scenes until it was time to stand-in for Ms. Sophie on Brewster's Place.

> All I would tell people is to hold on to what was Individual about themselves, not to allow their ambition for success, cause them to try to imitate the success of others, you've got to find it on your on terms.
> **-By Harrison Ford**

Meeting **_Iyanla Vanzant_** is something that I take no credit for. *She produced the "Iyanla Fix My Life," television show.* This opportunity is all my daughter's doing. She was invited to go to Oprah studio to be a part of a taping that was about a young man who had 34 children. This was definitely a time of learning how to seize the moment.

IYANLA VANZANT

I quickly ran in the hallway and asked if I could take a picture and to let her know that I was a big fan. I also pitched her a show idea that she wanted to use, we'll see what happens.

> The breakfast of champions is not cereal, it's the opposition.
> **-By Nick Seitz**

Shoot for the moon
even if you miss it,
you will land amongst
the Stars.
-By Les Brown

SINGER SEAL

To become so wrapped
up in something, that
you forget to be afraid.
-By Lady Bird Johnson

This was a very crazy night! I was on the scene when the famous *Rapper, Notorious B.I.G* was murdered in 2007. *He was an American New York rapper and songwriter whose one of the greatest rappers of all time.* In the photo above, I sat in **THE CARTOON CHARACTER'S, FRED FLINT-STONE MOBILE** for a photo opportunity. This photo further solidify my presence at the Auto Museum during the Vibe Magazine private party. This is where it all began after the Soul Train Award Show of which I was invited by a friend.

It was with great excitement, meeting all the stars (people that I watched on TV for years). I began taking pictures with them so that I could show my friends and family once I returned home. This was also on a road to the beginning of a journey that I had never taken before. The bottom photo on this page is of the *Famous Singer Seal* and I. *He's a British singer and songwriter who sold over 20 million records world wide and more.*

RUSSELL SIMONS

COMEDIAN TK CARTER

The famous Notorious Big was sitting next to *Russell Simons* and I while we were posing for this photo. *Russell is an American entrepreneur, record executive, writer and film producer and Hip Hop music label, Def Jam Recording and created Phat Farm fashion line.* Who knew that this was the last time that Biggy would be alive.

I got mad in this moment because Biggy's bodyguards wouldn't let him take a picture with me so Russell stood up instead to not leave me hanging.

Tk Carter was there that night too. *He's an American comedian and actor whose most known for many comedic performances and was nominated for the Naacp Image Award as an outstanding actor in a television movie.*

During my teen years, TK played in a lot of comedy shows. His latest tv movie that he played in was **the Bobby Brown Story**.

LISA (LEFT EYE) LOPEZ

This photo of *TLC's Left-eye* and I was taken at the Soul Train award show. *TLC is an American girl group formed in Atlanta in the 1990's, scoring nine top-ten hits on the Billboard Charts and the first R&B group in history receiving honor from the Recording Industry Association of America and lots more.* This was my second time going to Hollywood with my girlfriends, Kyshia Smith and Wendy from Dudley's Beauty College. In this moment of life, I also received my cosmetology license because while waiting to get discovered in show business, I had to have a way to make money other than doing waitress work.

Never let go of that fiery sadness called desire.
-By Patti Smith

Necessity and discontent are basic motivators! Necessity who is the mother of our invention.
-By Plato

This photo of *Tyler Perry* and I was taken at **Steve Harvey's Hoodie Awards** in Las Vegas which was changed to the Neighborhood Awards (to highlight excellence in African American Communities). *Tyler is an American actor, director, producer and screenwriter, listed as the highest paid man in entertainment for popularizing the image of an elderly black woman called Madea and now owns one of largest movie studios in the United States.* I was so excited to finally meet Tyler Perry and do believe that one day, I'll be working with him. A friend invited me to this event and every since, I 'd attend yearly to meet and interview other stars because around this time, I started my own my local tv show.

TYLER PERRY

Seen here is _Jennifer Hudson_, her baby boy and I. *She's an American singer, actress and philanthropist and has been the recipient of numerous accolades including an Oscar for her breakout role in "Dream Girls." To date she has the EGOT status, having won all 4 of the most prestigious awards in Entertainment (an Emmy, Grammy, Oscar and Tony).*

JENNIFER HUDSON

I have a touching story to tell you regarding her family in connection to our local tv show. Some of my youth members that I began working with was responsible for helping to kick off a charitable foundation in honor of her nephew, **Julian King.** Her younger cousin *Starlet Windom* was also our child abuse prevention spokesperson and singer, so many great memories.

> # I want to do it because I want to do it.
> ### -By Amelia Earhart
>
> # Friendships aren't perfect and yet they are precious for me not expecting perfection all in one place was a great release.
> ### -By Letty Cottin Pogrebin

COMEDIAN

ADELE

GIVENS

We grew up knowing _Adele Givens_ from the west side of Chicago. *She's also known as an American comedian actress and writer.*

Who knew that she was going to be a famous person one day. This is what I'm talking about, you don't know what's in your path. It's a good thing to get words of wisdom especially from people who've been where you are trying to go. I promise you, IT HELPS!

Seen here is the great legendary singer *Shirley Murdock*. **She** *is an American R&B singer-songwriter, who is best known for her 1986 R&B hit single, "As We Lay," and others. Lord have mercy, she sings one of those convicting songs called "As We Lay").* Unfortunately, it reminds me of how my husband and I got back together. Our story will be further explained in my other book called *"In the House with a King."* I finally got a chance to meet her in person. This photo was taken at Jennifer Hudson's family's funeral.

SHIRLEY MURDOCK

I ran into *Tamar Braxton*. *She is an American singer and television personality, a member of the Braxtons, an R&B singing group formed with her sisters with superstar, Tony Braxton being her sister and mentor.*

TAMAR BRAXTON

I did watch their reality show " The Braxton Family Values." I saw her on a promotional tour. Tamar was a lot of fun. She talked about her career and being a mom of which she states that it's not easy at times. Here's another reason why encouraging positive words are very important because stars get discouraged at times too.

Here's Mr. Johnny Gill and I. He's an American singer, songwriter and actor. Gill is the sixth and final member of the R&B/pop group New

JOHNNY GILL

Edition and was also a member of the supergroup called LDG with Gerald Levert and Keith Sweat. Yep, that's right, one of the greatest singers from the New Edition.

This photo opportunity was taken backstage at the Black Women's Expo. I was setting up our props to model for our new 50 campaign and they came rushing him in for a sound check and he stopped to meet me and pose for this photo.

Failure is only an opportunity to begin more intelligently. -By Henry Ford

Aaron Hall is an American recording artist, songwriter and record producer. Hall rose to prominence in 1988 as a member of the R&B and New Jack Swing group, called GUY which he founded in the late 80s along with Teddy Hall and Damion Hall.

AARON HALL

He was very nice and pleasant to meet. His music group was another staple in our childhood. My husband and I was invited to their concert in Chicago. I'm also a big fan of his brother who preaches the gospel, **Todd Hall**. I now finally got a chance to meet the brother, *Pastor Hall* often talks about while preaching his sermons, oh wow!

What worries you, masters you. -By Haddon W. Robinson

The test of enjoyment is the, remembrance which it leaves behind. -By J.C.F Von Schiller

You may know this Actor Comedian **_Tommy Davidson_** *from the 90s tv show, "In Living Color" and a host of other production projects. Tommy is an American comedian, film and television actor.*

I ran into him along with so many other celebrities during Steve Harvey's Neighborhood Awards in Las Vegas. Tommy has no shut off button when it comes to being naturally funny. He's always ready to make you laugh.

TOMMY
DAVIDSON

Most folks are about as happy as they make up their minds to be. -By Abraham Lincoln

MUSIQ
SOULCHILD

*Musiq
Soulchild,*

an American singer and song-writer whose style blends, R&B, funk, blues, jazz, gospel influences fused with hip hop.

This photo was also taken at Steve Harvey's Neighborhood Awards. He was also just as excited to be in the room with some of the other celebrities like I was. This let me know that stars can be star struck too (lol).

When and If you decide to become an Actress or Actor, you will have to get a professional headshot done.

My very first professional head shot was taken by the late great world renown _Ernest Collins._ _He was a famous fashion and make-up photo artist in the business that elevated black beauty like no other._ A head shot is like your personal ID for the show business world. It always has to be updated to show them what you look like to date.

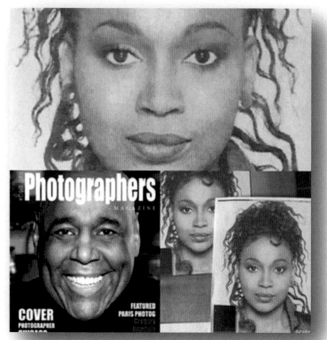

ERNEST COLLINS

God has entrusted me with myself. -By Epictertus

This is definitely a familiar face. _Kym Whitley_ _is one of the funniest Actresses and Comedian_ _that I know. She is best known for her roles on_ _tv sitcoms, such as Animal Practice, the_ _Parkers, Ice Cubes Friday Movies and_ _more._ This photo was also taken at the Neighborhood awards.

KIM WHITLEY

When you blame others, you give up your power to change. -By Anon

ESTER ROWE

Whenever you see me wearing this dress in a photo, it was on the same night that I was invited in my role as a beauty Queen at the NAACP IMAGE AWARDS.

I was definitely star struck when I met my childhood tv mom, **Actress** _Ester Rowe from the very popular long running comedy series, "Good Times."_ She 's best known for her role as Florida Evans, the character she played on two 1970's sitcoms; Maude in 1972 and Good Times in 1974. She was very sweet in person.

There are three ingredients in the good life: learning, earning and yearning. -By Christopher Morley

Damion Hall is an American R&B singer. He is also a member of the new jack swing group called GUY and is another brother of Aaron Hall.

He is also related to the Pastor that I love to hear preach, Dr. Todd Hall, as told on a previous page. The Group performed close to my house one summer night and my husband and I was invited to meet them backstage for a potential musical partnership.

Nobody holds a good opinion of a man who has a low opinion of himself. -By Anthony Trollope

TEDDY RILEY

To love others, we must first learn to love ourselves.
-By Anon

This person is the last of the widely popular music group GUY. His name is *Teddy Riley an American singer, songwriter, record producer and multi-instrumentalist credited with the creation of the new jack swing genre.* In fact, he just got his Hollywood Walk of Fame Star in California cemented in the ground for his genius work as the super producer of the music group.

He talked to my husband, (*Farley Jackmaster Funk, the King of House Music*) about working on a project. It would be nice to see House Music and Teddy Riley's hip hop with the New Jack Swing style come together for some great hits.

OMG! Who remembers this legendary singer that had his daughters backing him up; It's the late *Mr. Pops Staples* along with his children Mavis, Pervis Yvonne and Cleotha Staples. The group is known as the Staples Singers and I met them during my reign as a beauty winner, Ms Mahagony. *The Staples Singers was an American gospel and R&B pivotal figure from the 60s and 70s, Pops Staples was also a guitarist.*

POPS STAPLES

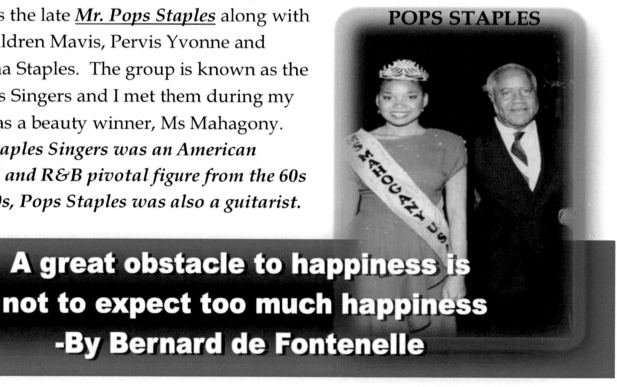

A great obstacle to happiness is not to expect too much happiness
-By Bernard de Fontenelle

We cannot all be masters!
-By William Shakespeare

My, My My, what do I say about this young lady right here. One of the most talented Actresses that I know, _Kimberly Elise._ _She's known as an American film and television actress and received critical acclaim for her performance in the movie Beloved and more._ This photo opportunity was taken at the Black Women's Expo in Chicago. She was promoting her new haircare products and still took the time to stop and take a picture with me.

KIMBERLY
ELISE

Cassie Davis is a long time Actress who works on mostly all of Tyler Perry productions. I met her when she was working on Tyler's House of Payne, a very funny sitcom. We are posing for this photo at the Neighborhood Awards. Her energy was just as exciting that night as it was watching her on television.

CASSY DAVIS

The Work Praises the Man.
-By Iris Proverb

Oscar Winner/Comedian <u>Monique Angela Hicks</u>, known professionally as Mo'Nique. She's an American stand-up comedian and actress that has received various accolades including the Oscars.

He turns not back who is bound to be a star.

-By Leonardo Divinci

In this photo, we were also at the Neighborhood Awards. She ended up giving me a short interview to encourage Kids in my youth group, called Kidz Korna. She is really funny and very witty on her toes.

EDDIE

GRIFFIN

Vision is the art of seeing things invisible. -By Jonathan Swift

Meeting *<u>Mr. Eddie Griffin</u>, Actor and Popular Comedian was another WOW moment.*

When this photo of he and I was taken during the Soul Train Music Awards, all I could think about was the very funny movies that he played in. He also played opposite of Dave Chapelle, Lady Gaga and Bradley Cooper in 2018's Academy Award Winning feature film. A Star is Born and lots more.

> ## It is enough that I am of Value to some body today.
>
> ### -By Hugh Prather

This photo of the **young _Ray J_** was at the soul train awards. He's the brother of the award winning recording artist and actress Brandy.

Ray J's professionally known as _an American Singer, Songwriter, Rapper, Tv Personality, Actor and Entrepreneur._ At this time, he was just around 17 years old, I took this photo of him.

RAY J

> ## We all live with the directive of being happy, Our lives are different and yet the same.
> ## -By Anne Frank

ANTHONY HAMILTON

This was another night at the Steve Harvey's Neighborhood Awards.

In this moment, I had an opportunity to interview _Mr. Anthony Hamilton. He's an American Singer Songwriter and record producer who rose to fame with his platinum-selling second studio album._

On the set of Jo Jo Dancer w/Richard Pryor Delece & other Actresses

In this photo, we are on the set of the Late **_Richard Pryor's_**, Jo Jo Dancer movie. The other two ladies seen here were also aspiring actresses.

Working on any set, whether filming a movie or television show, there will be a lot of unused time. There will also be a collective group of activities to bring scenes, people, equipment and props together. Either, you start out as a extra, doing background work or be blessed enough to catch a big break by landing a role, it's still fascinating to see how the

Delece on the Set of Jo Jo Dancer
she played a waitress in Richard Pryor's Movie

final outcome comes together with all the moving parts behind the scenes. In fact, this is how I got my waitress role. Richard Pryor elevated me by picking me over the other girls. It was an very exciting time!

Who knows where your path will lead. Seen here is *Jada Pinkett Smith, the American actress, screenwriter, producer, talk show host, businesswomen and an occasional singer-songwriter and wife to the world famous Will Smith.*

JADA PINKETT SMITH

She began her acting career in 1990. Jada has worked in many of my favorite television sitcoms of our teen years. She recently had a widely popular Facebook show called the Red Table Talk. This photo was also taken at the Soul Train Awards, the year that I attended with my good friend named *Princess Hemphill*.

QUINCY JONES & BRIAN MCKNIGHT

Seen here in this photo is a glimpse of *Quincy Jones whose career spans over 60 years in the entertainment industry with a record 80 Grammy award nominations, 28 Grammys and a Legend Award in 1992.*

Brian McKnight is a singer, song-writer, actor, arranger, record producer and multi-instrumentalist. His face is up front.

The Late MERRI DEE

Merri Dee *is an author, former tv journalist, and American philanthropist. She's best known for her work at Chicago Illinois television* **station** *and national cable superstation WGN-TV as an anchor/reporter from 1972 until 1983 and director of community relations until 2008. Many of us knew her as the Powerball host for many years on Channel 09.* We took this photo at a public event for the **former Mayor of Chicago, Mayor Richard M. Daley**.

This photo is a picture of reality star and ex-wife to the famous singer-songwriter R. Kelly. Her name is **_Andrea Kelly_**. She is **_an American choreographer, dance and actress._** We posed for this photo before all of the misfortunate incidents happened with her ex-husband. What I can tell you about meeting her, is that she's a very spiritual person. In fact she was praying for someone this night. I do believe that her faith in God will see her and her children through their difficult time.

ANDREA KELLY

KEANU

REEVES

I worked with this movie star, *Keanu Reeves, a Canadian actor, who began acting in theatre productions and in television films. One of his most popular acting roles was in the Movie called Matrix. His character's name was Neo. This was an extremely popular movie in the 90's.*

The movie that I worked with him on was called **Hardball** which was filmed in Chicago.

Good friends, good books and a sleepy conscience: this is the ideal life. -By Mark Twain

I didn't mind working as an extra because at any given moment you could get upgraded to receiving a principle role. A speaking part or a major role, is something that can definitely shift your career very fast. Again, this is what happened to me in the Richard Pryor movie. Richard picked me on the spot that bumped up my acting position which was a blessing,

Delece on the set of Hard Ball she played with Keanu Reeves

because to get a major role this way is very slim and so competitive. This photo was taken on the set of the Hardball movie.

I always thought I should be treated like a star. -By Madonna

This is a scene from the movie, *"Weird Science,"* which was produced by the famous director *John Hughes. He's an American filmmaker, beginning his career in 1970 as an author of humorous essays and stories for the National Lampoon Magazine.*

WEIRD SCIENCE MOVIE

Stars in this movie includes <u>*Robert Downing Jr, Kelly LeBrook, Anthony Michael Hall and Ilan Mitchell-Smith.*</u>

You can see me here standing behind **Robert Downing Jr** in the mall scene and some of the other scenes went to the editor's floor.

> # We must make the best of those ills which cannot be avoided.
> # -By Alexander Hamilton

This is not Delece's photo

GLADYS KNIGHT

This is a photo of the beautiful <u>*Gladys Knight*</u>. Her singing career spans over fifty years. *She's known as one of the greatest very few singers with unassailable artistry. This seven–time Grammy winner has enjoyed #1 hits in Pop, Gospel, R&B and Adult contemporary, and has triumphed in film, television and live performances that also included her in the music group, Gladys Knight and the Pips.*

> ## Optimism is the faith that leads to achievement. Nothing can be done without hope and confidence.
> ## -By Helen Keller

DA BRAT

I invited my associate (Wendy) to visit the Soul Train Awards along with my friend Kyshia Smith. This photo was taken back stage with Shawntae Harris better known by her stage name *Da Brat whose 1994 album "Funkdafied," made her the first female rapper to go platinum and more.*

Striving for success without hard work is like trying to harvest where you haven't planted.
-By David Bly

The thing about show business is that mostly every job is temporary; from modeling, to acting, to the music. So, until you get your big break, you may struggle in between and all of these stars got some serious stories to tell, regarding their hustle.

TISHA CAMPBELL

What can I say about *Tisha Campbell whose most known for Martin's girlfriend Gina in the Martin Lawrence 90s sitcom. The longevity of her singing and acting career is very impressive.* Often many people would compare my smile to hers. It was so great to finally meet her in person.

To dream too much of the person you would like to be is to waste the person you are.
-By Anon

If something doesn't come out the way you want, you have to forge ahead anyway.
-By Clint Eastwood

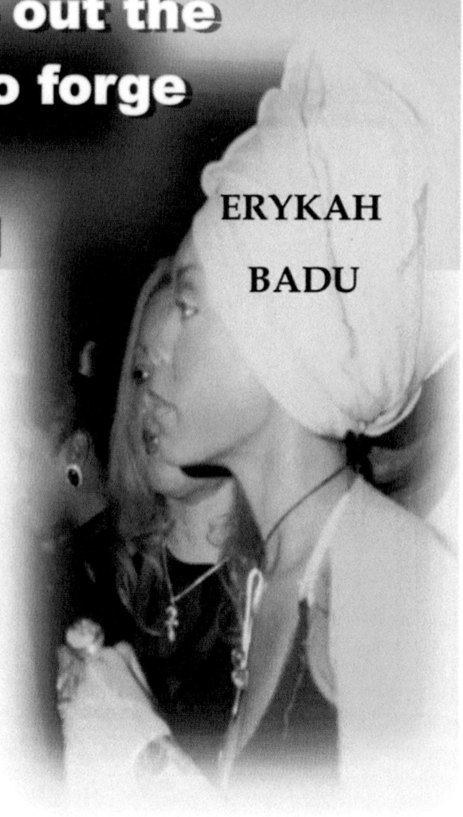
ERYKAH BADU

Erykah Badu ***is an American singer-songwriter, record producer and actress, influenced by R&B, 1970s soul and 1980s hip hop. Badu became associated with the Neo soul subgenre in the 90s and 2000s along with artist like D'Angelo. She has been called the Queen of Neo soul and is currently DJing.*** She is seen here at the Soul Train Awards. A lot of these talented people where on the brink of stardom at that time.

Paris and I posed for this photo opportunity in the backyard of the Jackson's childhood home in Gary Indiana. I was given the pleasure of being the only person to film Michael's children while they where visiting Michael and his sibling's elementary and high schools. I now cherish that footage and am thankful for this moment in time. I felt a little closer to our childhood superstar by being in the presence of his family.

MICHAEL JACKSON'S DAUGHTER PARIS

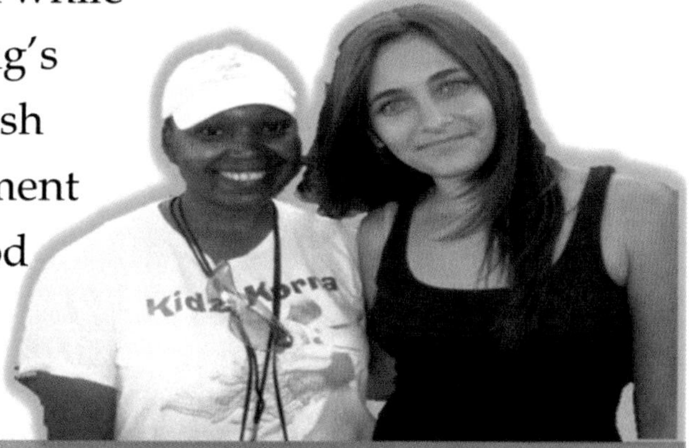

We must constantly build dykes of courage to hold back the flood of fear.
-By Martin Luther King Jr.

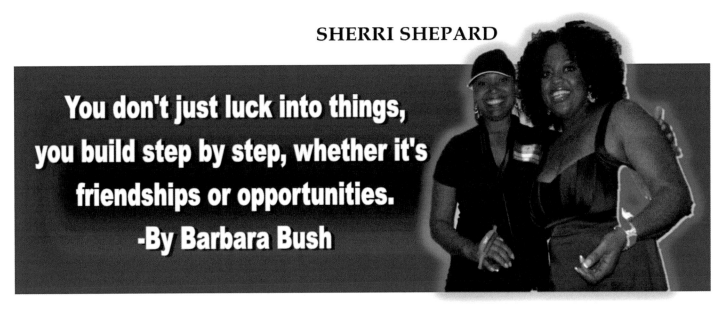

You don't just luck into things, you build step by step, whether it's friendships or opportunities.
-By Barbara Bush

Seen above is a photo of *Sherri Shepard* and I. It's also during the television interviews at Steve Harvey's Neighborhood awards in Las Vegas. *She is an American actress, comedian, author and television personality. Sherri was co-host of the daytime talk show, "The View" for which she received multiple Daytime Emmy nominations, winning one in 2009.* Sherri now has her own national day time talk show.

Bloom where you are planted!
-By Anon

DR. T'KEYAH CRYSTAL KEMAH

Remember this Disney Mom in the photo below? Her name is *Dr. T'Keyah Crystal Keymah. She is an American actress and singer, in addition to her status as an original cast member of the Fox sketch comedy series "In Living Color. Other acting jobs she had was in the Cosby Show and the most popular Disney Channel sitcom, "That's So Raven.* Whenever Dr. T'Keyah comes back to Chicago, she has often supported our youth program and more. She's seen here taking a picture with my late aunt Willien, definitely fun times.

PATRICE RUSHON

Those who trust to chance must abide by the results of chance. -By Calvin Coolidge

Patrice Rushen is an American jazz pianist and R&B singer. She is also a composer, record producer, multi-instrumentalist, songwriter and music director. She received Grammy nominations for her songs, "Forget Me Nots," as Best Female R&B Vocal Performance and others. This photo was taken at the Naacp Image Awards.

I also ran into Uncle Charlie professionally known as _Charlie Wilson_. He's been nominated for thirteen Grammy awards and ten NAACP Image Awards (including two wins). He was named Billboard magazine's No. 1 Adult R&B Artist, and his song, "There Goes My Baby." He was also named the No. 1 Urban Adult Song in Billboard Magazine.

CHARLIE WILSON

Begin somewhere; you can not build a reputation on what you intend to do. -By Liz Smith

KANDI
BURRUSS

If you watch reality tv, then you should know this young lady from the Real House Wives of Atlanta, *Kandi Burrus Tucker*. *She's also a singer, songwriter, television actress and business woman. Burrus first gained notoriety in 1992 as a member of the female vocal group, Xscape.*

I met up her and her Mom *Joyce Jones* (seen here in this photo). They were a bunch of fun beautiful ladies to interview for our Kidz Korna local tv show. We met them at this event in Chicago while Kandi was promoting her products.

JOYCE JONES

HOWARD
HEWETT

This is a photo of the man whose gospel song called, *"SAY AMEN,"* literally changed my life. Never in a million years that I'd think to meet him in person to tell him about it. <u>*Howard Hewett*</u> *is a Grammy Award-winning American songwriter. He rose to fame as lead vocalist of the Grammy winning R&B/soul vocal group Shalamar. Mr. Hewett has a discography documenting albums and singles full of top hits.* It was a sure pleasure to meet him at our friend's Gala with the IMAG Project.

Below is a photo of singer <u>*Fantasia Barrino*</u> *whose professionally known as an American R&B singer, songwriter, actress and author. She rose to fame as winner of the third season of the reality tv series American Idol in 2004.* I met Fantasia in Harvey IL. She performed with gospel recording artist Grammy winning **VaShawn Mitchell** that night during his street naming ceremony and concert.

FANTASIA
BURRINO

REVEREND
JESSE
JACKSON
SR

The *Reverend Jesse Jackson Sr.* and I was seen here upon our programs getting ready to participate in the Bud Billiken Parade. The Largest African American Parade in the United States. *Reverend Jackson is a civil rights Activist, Politician, Baptist Minister who also walked side by side with Dr. Martin Luther King Jr and still strongly carries on his legacy today. He was a candidate for the Democratic presidential nomination in 1984 and 1988 and served as a shadow U.S. Senator for the District of Columbia and so much more.*

REVEREND JESSE JACKSON'S WIFE
JACQUELINE BROWN JACKSON

I met *Mrs. Jackson* at an event for the Chicago State University students. I truly admire her beauty inside and out, her longevity and loyalty to her husband's vision and mission. Mrs. Jackson has also been a strong tower for her community and family.

DR. WILLIE WILSON

The purpose of life is a life of purpose. -By Robert Byrne

This man has a heart of gold. *Dr. Willie Wilson is a philanthropist, businessman and politician from Chicago. He later received a Doctor of Divinity degree from Mt. Carmel Theological Seminary and a Doctor of Humane Letters. He's currently owner of Omar Inc.*

He was very generous to our youth organization on several occasions. Kidz Korna's young people needed to be sponsored in order to participate in the Bud Billiken Parade and Dr. Wilson stepped up to cover the expenses. One year, our bus broke down during one of our busy seasons for delivering donations to families around the city and paid to get the bus repaired. His list is miles long for generously assisting others and we're proud of him for considering the least of them.

Meeting *Mrs. Katherine Jackson* was such a delight. Annually, she tries to come back to their childhood home in Gary Indiana to see how her son Michael's legacy is being celebrated by many of his fans from around world on his birthday. This photo was taken there.

MICHAEL JACKSON'S MOM KATHERINE JACKSON,

Great minds have purposes, others have wishes. -By Washington Irving

LISA RAYE - *Actress, Model, businesswoman & Fashion Designer.*

At this time, my friend Kyshia Smith seen behind *Lisa Raye* and I were excited to run into someone from Chicago. We were back stage at the Soul Train Awards. Almost all of the stars were from California, New York and other cities. It's nothing like seeing a person become as successful as any other person in they own right, from our hometown, Chicago.

Lisa Raye *was the Star of the movie Player's Club*. I remember being in a beauty pageant with her in my early 20's. As a young lady trying to discover my destiny, that beauty pageant experience meant a lot to me and I've learned a lot about myself by being in it. I will further discuss the details regarding this experience in my next book.

Seen here next to me, is the *award winning singer, songwriter and actress* _Faith Evans_, *a multi-platinum Grammy Award winning recording artist and autism awareness advocate.* She's also the wife of the Late **Rapper Notorious BIG**. She's holding their son Christopher Wallace here. This photo was also taken the night Biggy was murdered.

FAITH EVANS

HOLLY ROBINSON-PEETE

It's a painful thing to look at your own trouble and know that you, yourself and no one else, has made it.   -By Sophocles

This dynamic woman *Holly Robinson-Peete is an American actress and singer. She is known for her roles in 21 Jump Street, a sitcom with Mr. Cooper and lots more.* She and her husband, former NFL quarterback, *Rodney Peete* formed the HollyRod Foundation and they are dedicated to providing compassionate care to those living with Autism and Parkinson's disease. I am glad to have been in the presence of so many beautiful, successful and inspiring people whose also doing great things for their communities. This is another photo moment at Steve Harvey's Neighborhood Awards.

How old were you when you watched the movie, **"Cooley High?"** This movie is an all time classic for our generation and is timeless for generations to come. Who would have known that I would get a chance to meet one of the Characters, *Jackie Taylor*. *To date, she runs her own theater called the Black Ensemble and produces plays.* She allowed me to bring our youth program Kidz Korna there to bless the community with our annual toy giveaway event during the Covid Pandemic.

JACKIE TAYLOR

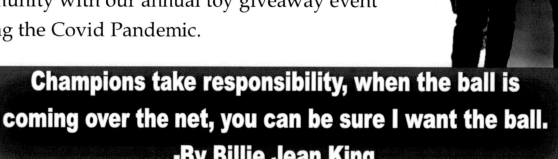

Champions take responsibility, when the ball is coming over the net, you can be sure I want the ball.
-By Billie Jean King

BRANDY

Think you can, think you can't,
either way, you'll be right.
-By Henry Ford

Wow! This is the one and only Brandy Rayana Norwood, better known by _Brandy_. *She's an American singer, songwriter, record producer, actress and businesswomen. Her career began with backing vocalist for teen groups as she was already born into a musical family. My favorite memory of Brandy is the role she portrayed in the 90's sitcom called Moesha. Until this day, my grand daughters loves all of the show's re-runs.*

The photo above was taken at the Soul Train Awards backstage along with meeting all of the other celebrities who performed that night. As soon as I approached Brandy and asked to take a photo with her, she gloated with a big smile and said, WOW! You are beautiful! There we were, both cheesing from ear to ear while I standing in the midst of all the excitement of being in the company of great people.

This is a photo of *Keenen Ivory Wayans. He comes from a family of great comedian siblings with many movies under their belt. Their brake out sitcom was called, "In Living Color."* This photo of us was taken at the BET Awards.

KEENEN
IVORY
WAYANS

I do not believe in
pessimism.
-By Clint Eastwood

The way a man's mind runs is the way he is sure to go.
-By Henry B. Wilson

DREW SIDORA

This American actress and singer is known for her recurring role as Chantel in the Disney Channel original series That's So Raven, also as Lucy Avila in the 2006 movie Step Up and starred as Tionne Watkins in the VH1, TLC biographical film called CrazySexyCool. She was also just recently cast in the Real House Wives of Atlanta, a reality television show. <u>Drew Sidora</u> and I took this photo at one of largest family picnic's in the city of Chicago and I am now friends with her older sister **Allison Jordan** who had a Arts and Entertainment studio for youth and families.

I met this young man name, Wasalu Muhammad Jaco, better known as <u>Lupe Fiasco</u>. *He's an American rapper, record producer, entrepreneur and activist. He rose to fame in 2006 following the success of his debut album, Lupe Fiasco's Food and Liquor.* I ran into him at this business meeting. He was taking the time to empower Chicago's youth by giving back.

LUPE FIASCO

As a man thinketh, so is he, and as a man chooseth, so is he.
from the Bible.

LAVAN
DAVIS

LaVan Davis is an American singer, comedian and actor best known for portraying the character Curtis Payne in Tyler Perry's House of Payne sitcom. I met him at Steve's Harvey's Neighborhood awards in Las Vegas. He also gave a public shout-out to my husband on the success of his music career.

ON THE SET OF THE MALCOLM X MOVIE

This photo was taken on the set of *Malcolm X*. There where several movie versions produced of the *American Muslim minister and human rights activist who was a popular figure during the civil rights movement.* I was hired to play a house wife/supporter of the Malcolm X movement. In the movie, I was sitting on the front row when Malcolm got shot. This was the outfit they dressed me up in.

GINA RAVERA

Gina Ravera is one of the original actresses in the break out film called Soul Food. She also co-starred as detective Irene Daniels in TNT's crime series,

The Closer and more. The film, "Showgirls" that she played in was one of my favorite educational movies, showing us why we shouldn't always idolize stars. They are just human beings who are given opportunities to shine and we are no different. This is why we need to do all that we can to be prepared when opportunities come our way as well. In the movie, her character got raped. I wasn't pleased with the rapist actions though but, it was only just a movie.

This is one popular face, *Mr. Joe Jackson, the Father to the all time greatest entertainer, Michael Jackson. He was an American talent manager and patriarch of the Jackson family of entertainers. He's also inducted into the Rhythm and Blues Music Hall of Fame.*

JOE JACKSON

Every saint has a past, and every sinner has a future.
-By Oscar Wilde

These news anchors work for the ABC Channel 07 network in Chicago. Throughout the years, Channel 07 would give my youth group news coverage regarding various projects that we did in communities. Each year, they would also invite me to their private empowerment luncheon for Black History month. I learned so much from others when I attend. This photo was taken there.

CHERYL BURTON

HOSEA SANDERS

MANCOW

This man has literally been on the Chicago scene for years with a personality that's huge in the market of radio and television. I finally get a chance to meet _Mancow_ from WLS. He interviewed my husband on this morning. I'll tell you more about my husband later.

Ask yourself the secret of your success. Listen to your answer, and practice it.
-By Richard Bach

JIM ROSE

Jim Rose is the sports anchor from ABC Channel 07. He, Cheryl Burton and Hosea Sanders has been there for over 20 years. I can remember at one point working on a movie project with Cheryl Burton.

She was a cheerleader in this movie called Lucas, and I was just a extra, sitting in the football stands as a fan of the game. Who knew that Cheryl would go on to get her big break and become a News Anchor. This is just a testament of what God can do. Every time I see her on tv, a young lady from the Southside of Chicago, who now sits in that seat is encouragement for me to keep believing in my dreams. Jim Rose just announced his retirement from Channel 07. We wish him well.

MELISSA FOREMAN & JEANE SPARROW

Melissa Forman and Jeanne Sparrow were co-host on Fox News show called You and Me this Morning. My husband and I were invited there for a televised interview as well.

Do it big or stay in bed!
-By Larry Kelly

JUDGE MATHIS

Judge Mathis is a long-running, Daytime Emmy Award-winning syndicated arbitration-based reality court show presided over by the retired Judge of Michigan's 36th District Court and black-culture motivational speaker. If you haven't heard about how he turned his life around while once serving time in prison, you really need to take some time to do so. Judge Mathis is a perfect example of what it takes to never give up on yourself. This photo was taken at Steve Harvey's Neighborhood Awards and he also gave me an interview to air on our local Kidz Korna tv show.

Below is a photo of NBC news anchor **Mr. Art Norman**. *He's also a long running news anchor of the network, won many prestigious awards for his journalist work and a very compassionate person to help strengthen communities.* You can always find Mr. Norman uplifting or mentoring aspiring journalist.

ART NORMAN

Morale is the greatest single factor in successful wars.
-By Dwight D. Eisenhower

JACKEE HARRY

Energy can do anything that can be done in this world. -By Johann von Goethe

We were on the set of Channel 07's Windy City Live television show. The main host **Val Warner** was absent so, the very talented _Jackee Harry_ filled in for her. She's sitting between the other co-host *Ryan Chiaverini* and a co-host contributor. **Jackee Harry** *is an American actress, singer, comedian, director and television personality. She is best known for her roles as Sandra Clark, the sexy nemesis of Mary Jenkins (played by Marla Gibbs) in NBC TV series 227 and as Lisa Landry on the ABC. WB sitcom Sister, Sister.* That's me at the bottom.

This photo is of _Dean Richards_ and I. **He's an American film** *critic and entertainment reporter for WGN-TV and a long-time radio host for WGN in Chicago.* We posed next to a monumental moment during the Channel 09 taping. In this moment, they had Bozo tv show photos hanging in the hallway. It was my first ever tv appearance at their production studio. The Bozo show was a fun-filled adventure for Chicago's young people. I was only 7 years old when I made my special appearance. I often wondered what happened to that footage.

DEAN RICHARDS

Energry and Persistance conquer all things. -By Benjiman Franklin

It is the heart which experiences God, not the reason.
-By Blaise Pascal

YOLANDA ADAMS

There's sooo much to say about this world changing award winning gospel song bird. *Yolanda Adams* has endless trailblazing hits that has brought me through so many trails and tribulations. This is the part that many people get confused. Some people think that when you begin to trust God with your life, you are not supposed to go through many things, or you must not be a child of God if you are being attacked a lot. Well, the promises of God will let you know that what you go through in this life, he's always there to protect you and that's what her songs where for me. They where reassurances of God's protection for me anywhere and anytime of the day. *Yolanda is an American gospel singer, record producer, actress, and host of her own nationally syndicated morning gospel show. She sold nearly 10 million albums worldwide achieving multi-platinum status.*

SMOKIE NORFUL The *Reverend "Smokie" Norful Jr.* *is an American gospel singer and pianist, best known for his album, I Need You Now*. Seen here is my grand daughter Dior, we ran into him at the mall.

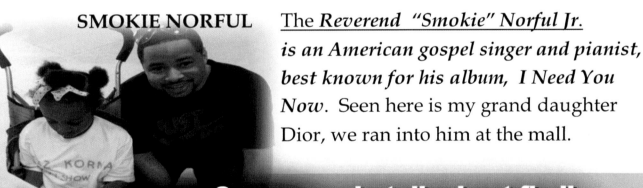

Some people talk about finding God, as if He could get lost.
-By Anon

TYE TRIBBETT

A consciousness of God releases the greatest power of all.
-By Science of Mind

I met the super cool and very talented _Tye Tribbett_ at one of his concerts in Chicago. *He's an American gospel music singer, songwriter and keyboardist. He is the choir director and founder of the Grammy nominated and Stellar Award-winning gospel group Tye Tribbett & G.A. Tye Tribbett has over 20 years in music and ministry and career sales exceeding 1.3 million units across (6) commercially released albums.*

In past generations, listeners could expect to see either a traditional choir or a quartet vocal group when it came to gospel music performances. However, much of today's gospel music is diverse and designed to reach people both inside and outside the church community; at church and at the club. Tye's goal is to offer something for everyone. He's best known for the exciting, high energy praise concerts orchestrated with Greater Anointing, his longtime group of vocalists and musicians. His fans have come to expect rousing singing, explosive dances and powerful testimonies.

This next photo is of _Pam Morris_ and I. *She's a gospel commentator who welcomes a lot of gospel groups to perform here in Chicago and more.*

PAM MORRIS

I believe in the incomprehensibility of GOD.
-By Honore de Balzac

MARY, MARY

Faith is a gift of God.
-By Blaise Pascal

Faith assuages, guides and
restores. -By Arthur Rimbaud

This very popular contemporary gospel duo called **Mary Mary** *are two* sisters *Erica Atkins-Campbell and Trecina Atkins-Campbell who where launched into mainstream recognition following the release of their best-selling debut album, Thankful in 2000. It also contained their hit single "Shackles (Praise You)." Mary Mary has sold more than eight million records worldwide to date. The duo have been nominated for eleven Grammy Awards, winning four times along with having many other hits. The group's name is inspired by two famous Marys' from the Bible: Mary, mother of Jesus, and Mary Magdalene. They also performed at the White House and lots more.* The photo above is of the group and I, and it was taken at V103's radio station when they where on their promotional tour.

Below is a photo of *Detrick Haddon*. I met him during the 79th street Renaissance Festival in Chicago. *He's a gospel singer, songwriter, music producer, pastor and actor. He is best known for progressive gospel and a contemporary style of music.*

DETRICK HADDON

To think you are separate from God is
to remain separate from your own being.
-By D.M. Street

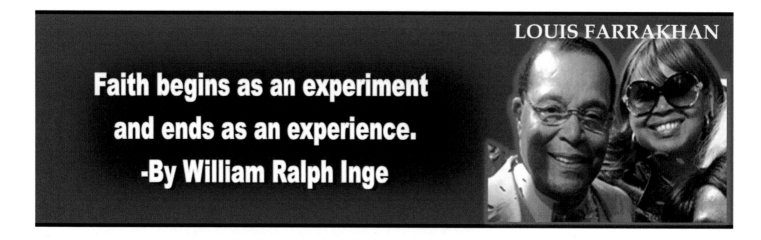

I was invited to one of <u>*Minister Louis Farrakhan's*</u> speaking engagements with my husband. We were able to sit on the stage directly behind him and the room looked different as the audience was truly engaged and hanging on to every word that he said. This was my first time ever hearing him speak in person. *He's known as Louis X, an American religious leader and political activist who heads the Nation of Islam. Earlier in his career, he was appointed National Representative of the Nation of Islam by former NOI leader Elijah Muhammad.*

The last photo on this page is with <u>*Pastor Darius Brooks*</u> and I. He has one particular song that is a timeless hit. It's called, "Your Will" which was released in 1999 but is still frequently played. *Mr. Brooks is an American gospel musician. He started his music career in 1990 with the release of, Simply Darius, by Sound of Gospel, and he would go on to release five more albums with his label imprint, Journey Music Group.*

DARIUS BROOKS For over three decades Darius has thrived in almost every music capacity and is now a pastor.

Let God love you through others and let God love others through you. -By D.M. Street

T.D. JAKES

BISHOP T.D JAKES, WIFE SHARITA JAKES, STATE REPRESENTATIVE SHELIA JACKSON, & JOEL OSTEEN'S MOM , DODIE OSTEEN

This is a photo of some powerful people that represents Politics, God's kingdom and lots more. I met them during **T.D Jake's Woman Thou Art Loosed Mega Conference.** I did not know that Bishop Jakes also allows his ministry platform to be a go to forum for everyone from Reality Stars to Rap Artist. I can now remember the time when there was much controversy surrounding Comedian Steve Harvey hosting, Jakes Megafest/Woman Thou Loosed Mega Conferences.

In the church world, there is lots of judgement calls on how saved you are (committed to living for the Lord and not the world), if you are very active in supporting or doing certain things in the world. Will God love you more or less according to your faithfulness in serving him? Here's the kicker, there are a lot of people who truly tributes their success to God because they know him. Some stars are faithful to paying tithes to the church even when they don't have the time to attend. More about this topic will be discussed in my books, stay tuned.

The kingdom of God is within you. -By Luke 17:21

MY SISTER, ANDRENA HILTIONEN AND I

REVEREND CLAY EVANS

Do I go or do I not go to church? Where else can you deeply learn about the things of God. This is why your relationship with this powerful spirit being is a heart matter more than a head matter. This is a topic for discussion in another one of my books, stay tuned to learn more in Volume 3.

Above, is a photo of the Famous _Late Reverend Clay Evans and I_. He died at the age of 94 years old. *He was an African American Baptist pastor and founder of the influential Fellowship Missionary Baptist Church in Chicago, Illinois. It's known for it's gospel music infused Sunday service and choir.*

Below is a photo of the beloved song bird, the _late Albertina Walker_. *She was an American gospel singer, songwriter, actress, and humanitarian and all time hero to many underserved young people with her scholarship benefit concerts. She has sooo many hits under her belt and she also sang with the Caravans group (Shirley Caesar, Dorothy Norwood and Inez Andrews).* She also has been associated with the great **Mahalia Jackson**. I have 2 hours of videotaped footage of her star studded homegoing celebration awaiting to be released on the Kidz Korna tv show.

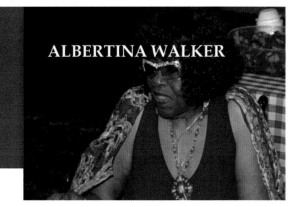

ALBERTINA WALKER

Faith is a higher faculty than reason. -By Bailey

After years of striving for success with my professional goals, I too realized having faith in God made my victories possible. In fact, one of my most convincing moments for believing that God was watching over me was when I worked on *Spike Lee's* movie called Jungle Fever. It took a whole lot of faith to go to New York alone with only thirty dollars in my pocket. I was so scared in this huge city, only to be blessed to stay in Spike Lee's sister apartment for free, for two weeks while using my bible as if it was a pillow to sleep on.

I ended up working on the set with *Actress Halle Berry, Isaiah Washington, Wesley Snipe and Ossie Davis and Ruby Dee.* Other details on FAITH will be discussed in volume 3 of my book, "**On The Shoulders of Giants Angels.**" On that note, my sister Andrena and I started our decade old daily early prayer line. We needed to seek God's wisdom in our day to day living since God has shown that he always has my back. Below is a photo of *Fred Hammond*. *This award winning gospel singer, song writer, producer has so many hits songs in his portfolio. He was a part of group called "Commissioned," and regarded as one of the most popular figures in contemporary gospel music.* I met him at a Bishop Jakes Conference.

Deep faith eliminates fear. -By Lech Walesa

FRED HAMMOND

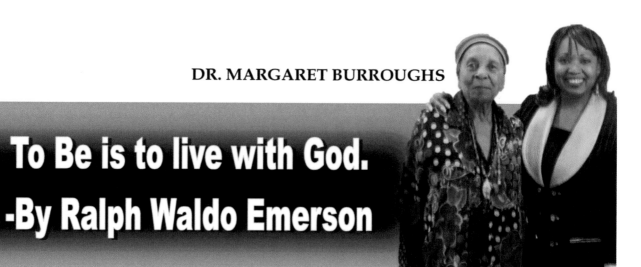

To Be is to live with God.
-By Ralph Waldo Emerson

Above, is a photo of **<u>Dr. Burroughs</u>** and I. *She is responsible for finding Chicago's Dusable Museum of African American History which is dedicated to the study and conservation of African-American history, culture and art, all from her home. Her unique art renderings tells you a story of faith, hope and love and you can find them in the Dusable Museum.* I met her at my friend's Women conference.

Below is **<u>Anthony Brown</u>** and I. He's from the popular gospel group called *Anthony Brown and group therAPy. They are an American urban contemporary gospel artist and musician. Mr. Brown was*

ANTHONY
BROWN

initially known as the go-to songwriter and vocal arranger for artists. Mr. Brown along with his group emerged as a breakthrough artist.

This photo was taken during a anti-violence ministry conference in Chicago.

Faith is the substance of things hoped for and the evidence of things not seen.
-By Hebrew 11:1

Public validation is important.
Be careful of those who can
only love you in private.
-By T. D Jakes

Above, is a photo of _Vashawn Mitchell_. *He is the American gospel singer who broke into fame with his massive hit single, "Nobody Greater." He has produced several Stellar Award-winning projects and songs for Grammy Award winners Vanessa Bell Armstrong and Smokie Norful.* I remember VaShawn as a seasoned singer, songwriter, producer and musical director at Sweet Holy Spirit Church. *In fact, he was serving at a pair of Chicago churches while nurturing a multi-faceted career and producing his own albums. He was later based in Atlanta and having chart-topping success which crossed over to the R&B market on subsequent releases, leading to ambitious projects like the 2016 album Secret Place, which he recorded in South Africa.*

Below is a photo of this trailblazing gospel producer, _Dana Devine._ She did something in the gospel arena that was so risking for the

DANA DEVINE

church world. *She created the Gospel Slide Song; a line dance style for group activity participation.* She received much push back at first but finally a break though, saints began to accept it.

He does not believe who does
not live according to his belief.
-By Thomas Fuller

FATHER MICHAEL PFLEGER

Faith is the proper name of religious experiences.
-By John Baillie

This famous activist and senior pastor at Saint Sabina is a leader in fighting against Chicago's Gun Violence. *Father Michael Pfleger is a Roman Catholic priest of the Archdiocese of Chicago. His social activism has brought him media coverage throughout the world and beyond. He has often collaborated and associated with African American religious, political and other social activists such as Jeremiah Wright, Joseph Lowery, Jesse Jackson, Harry Belafonte, Cornel West and Louis Farrakhan.* Under Pfleger's leadership, the community of St. Sabina demanded the shutdown of a number of Auburn Gresham businesses specializing in drug paraphernalia, removal of tobacco and alcohol billboards from their neighborhoods.

Pastor John Hannah is another Chicago minister who mostly influences the young people. He is a husband, speaker and author who's impacted his community in leading thousands to Christ with his once popular early morning radio show on Inspiration 1390 am in Chicago. He's seen here giving my husband an award for House Music.

To me, faith means not worrying.
-By John Dewey

PASTOR JOHN HANNAH

Page 54

Without pleasure, man would live like a fool and soon die.
-By Pierre de Beaumarchais

FARLEY JACKMASTER FUNK, KING OF HOUSE MUSIC

Love brought us here from a friendship of over 38 years. *On this page, I introduce to you, my best friend, husband and World Renown DJ/Music Producer who is famously known as one of the creators of a music genre called House Music.*

His stage name is *Farley Jackmaster Funk, the King of House Music.* We've been married now for 20 years and counting and to God be the glory.

Below is a photo of Farley and the *late Darryl Pandy who is responsible for taking House Music global with their massive hit, "Love Can't Turn." It is the first House Music song to land on the European charts, thus changing the history of dance music worldwide.*

DARRYL

Your wealth is where your friends are.
-By Plautus

Man's best support is a very dear friend. -By Cicero

I was so excited when Farley allowed me to travel with him throughout Europe during some of his work projects. This is a photo of he and I in London. I got a chance to visit Paris France, Finland, Ireland, Many parts of Europe, Liverpool, Manchester, Sheffield and other cities. In fact, one of my fond memories was actually seeing sheep and little lamb in real life.

Please make it a personal goal to do some traveling. There's nothing like seeing the world with your own eyes. See how people live in other countries and to see how ordinary people do some extraordinary things to change the world like my husband and his musically inclined group of friends. These are definitely moments to bestow for the rest of my life. Below is a photo of *the **Hotmix 5,** the very popular multi-cultural Dj group who's responsible for making House Music a House hold name on WBMX radio.*

HOTMIX 5 @ CITY HALL

MAYOR RAHM EMANUEL

MISSING FROM THE PHOTO KENNY JAMMIN JASON

Farley was also a part of this group. We are seen here with the **former Mayor of Chicago, Rahm Emanuel**.

He is lifeless that is faultless. -By a English Proverb

Kindess is the golden chain by which society is bound together.
-By Johann von Goethe

What a gathering on this day! Unity amongst many Chicago DJ's.

They are all posing for a photo opportunity centered around a great cause. It was a celebrity basketball game while raising money for needy youth and families. This event was lots of fun, including brotherhood empowerment.

Guess who they had as cheerleaders? Yep, myself along with around twelve other women who where long-time House Music lovers, some girlfriends and wives. They definitely need to make this an annual event.

Do not remove a fly from your friend's forehead with a hatchet.
-By a Chinese Proverb

In this photo with my husband, are some other forefathers of the music genre, Dj /Producer *Wayne Williams, former A&R Executive, founder of the Chosen Few Picnic and more, and Steve Silk Hurley, another Dj/ Producer whose resume of master remixing includes many great singers from Prince to CeCe Peniston and lots more.*

WAYNE & FARLEY

STEVE

I'd rather be a lampost in Chicago than a millionaire in any other city. -By William A. Hulbert

DERRICK BROWN

Seen here is a photo of iHeartMeda's *Derrick Brown* whose been *promoted as VP of Urban programming at V103 radio station in Chicago. He's helping to keep the longevity of House Music alive. Brown continues his 60th win as Chicago's top-rated station under his tenure. Derrick is a consummate professional, a trailblazer and one of the best programming minds in the business.*

Below is a photo of Robin Stone, better known by her stage name <u>*Robin S*</u>. *She is an American House Music singer and songwriter, who scored success in the 1990s with such it singles as "Show Me Love," and "Luv 4 Luv."*

If you judge people, you have no time to love them. -By Mother Terresa

She has had three number ones on the Billboard Hot Dance Club Play chart. I met her one night at an event. The following week, she was performing on BET representing House Music very well.

ROBIN S

**Prosperity makes friends, adversity tries them.
-By Publilus Syrus**

This photo here was taken during a media promotional tour of the Hotmix 5's Dj group's 35th year anniversary celebration campaign. Starting on the top left, some of the original multi-cultural members are *Mickey Mixin Oliver, Ralphi Rosario, Scott Smokin Silz including Farley. Kenny Jamin Jason* is missing from the picture. He couldn't make it this day when we where invited to be apart of Channel 07's Windy City Live tv taping, to commemorate their contribution and history pertaining to House Music's Popularity.

This group (*the American DJ team originating from Chicago, IL in which all of these original members were chosen by WBMX radio Program Director, Lee Michaels in 1981*) they also had other Hotmix 5 members that helped to push House Music to the incredible heights as we know it today. Other members are; *Julian Perez, Steve Hurley, Mike Wilson, Mario Diaz and Ed Crosby*. This photo below is also from Windy City Live. The Mascot was made and given as a gift to my husband. Here we are posing in front of the show's sign.

**The morning has gold in its mouth.
-By a German Proverb**

TONY ROSALES

A friend in need is a friend indeed.
-By Richard Graves

My husband's business partner **_Tony Rosales_** and I were sitting in the audience during the taping. *Tony is credited for working with Farley to pull together an amazing one of a kind, Hotmix 5, 35th year anniversary extravaganza which included over 60 DJ's and 30 artist.*

The never seen before Hotmix 5 event included 5 different stages for the Dj's and Artist to pay homage to each Hotmix 5's original member while bringing over 19,000 worldwide house heads to the McCormick Convention Center to help celebrate. This year, marks the groups 40 plus year anniversary and talks are currently circulating regarding another huge event, in fact they are currently planning their annual event now.

I finally got a chance to meet **_Screamin Rachael_**, *CEO of Trax Records and the Late Attorney, Jay B. Ross while hanging out with my husband. Trax Records was owned by the late Larry Sherman whose main contribution was to help with House Music's record distributions* and *Jay B. Ross was famously known for advising some of the most prominent from people in entertainment, from the late James Brown to Ray Charles, and he was also my husband's attorney.*

SCREAMIN RACHAEL

JAY B. ROSS

It is the soul's duty to be loyal to its own desires.
-By Rebecca West

To have no set purpose in one's life is harlotry of the will.
-By Stephen McKenna

LONNIE BUNCH

Since the start and history of House Music, we often find it's beginning to be very misconstrued. The number one question surrounding it's origins is "How did it really get started?" You may hear that it started in New York, or in London or you may have heard that it was started based on a particular gender lifestyle which leaves out sooo many other major contributors. House Music started in Chicago and it's now my husband's lifetime goal to set the record straight by creating the **International House Music Museum and Hall of Fame (IHMMHF).** Farley's main goal with this project is to make sure that every person's legacy is not forgotten who've had something to do with it's inception and to give supporters a place they can call home for the music genre.

Above, is a picture of *Lonnie Bunch* **and I**. He is the *Director of the Smithsonian Institution an American educator and historian. Bunch is the 14th Secretary of the Smithsonian Institution, the first African American and first historian to serve as head of the Smithsonian. He spent most of his career as a history museum curator and administrator.* I caught up with him while giving a speech on how he got started with the construction of Washington DC's Smithsonian African American Museum of History and Culture. Seen here is our very first meeting on

OUR MUSEUM MEETINGS

Everyone has a right to his own course of action.
-By Moliere

Page 61

the planning of the International House Music Museum and Hall of Fame (IHMMHF). Listening to Mr. Bunch's speech could not have come at a better time.

The word **"Faith,"** was one of his most valuable key points in his message while explaining how he got started which is what helped him through. Faith is definitely what we have to ride on as well in order to see Farley's dream of making his Museum a reality. Mr. Bunch gave us nuggets of wisdom and encouragement to just get started. *Faith in God* and Mr. Bunch's words of wisdom is what just helped my husband open the first ever House Music Store which is founded by the House Music Museum Foundation. The headquarters is now in Chicago and this is just the beginning.

The photos on this page are taken during our visit on a Washington DC tour which included visiting the Smithsonian African American Museum. Farley and a lot of Chicago DJ's are featured in it. The photo at the top is

FARLEY, KENNY, DELECE, JULIAN

of us praying on the State Capitol grounds. **Ray Anderson** and **Congressman Bobby Rush's assistant Ingrid Gavin** was our tour guide. In this photo, we are touring the White House, along with members of the Hotmix 5.

JABARI PARKER

Example has more followers than reason. -By Christian Bovee

Above is a photo of Basketball legend, _Jabari Ali Parker_ with my nephew _Keith Griffin_ who lives in Georgia. At this time, Keith worked with us on some Kidz Korna projects in Chicago. In the presence of greatness, are game changing mindset moments for young people to understand the importance of working hard, staying focused and going after their dreams.

Parker is an American professional basketball player who last played for the Boston Celtics of the National Basketball Association. He was selected by the Milwaukee Bucks with the second overall pick in the 2014 NBA draft, after one season of playing for Duke University.

A lot of my nephews are very fortunate to have many sports players as mentors because of my brother in law who lives in Orlando Florida. He cuts their hair and h_e's known as a Celebrity Barber to the stars._ Many of the athletes do not have a problem with spreading words of wisdom to young people because they know how fortunate they are to have become successful.

These are my original photos of superstar athlete _Dwayne Wade_. I was invited to his mom's church.

A conclusion is a place where you got tired of thinking. -By Fischer's Law

Example is not the main thing in influencing others, it is the only thing.
-By Albert Schweitzer

ANOTHER JABARI PARKER PHOTO OPPORTUNITY

Dwayne was the guest speaker that night. *He is an American former professional basketball player who spent the majority of his 16-year career playing for the Miami Heat in the National Basketball Association.* I had the opportunity to interview him as he was there to help kick off the opening of their community center that was being built as addition to the church. He shared his legacy and goals to inspire everyone in attendance with words of wisdom and more.

Below is a photo of superstar golfer _Tiger Woods_. *He is an American professional that tied for first in PGA Tour wins, ranks second in men's major championships and holds numerous gold records. Woods is widely regarded as one of the greatest golfers of all time and one of the most famous athletes of all time.*

TIGER WOODS

This is not Delece's Photo

Sherrod is my other nephew that had an opportunity to meet Tiger Woods because Tiger was another one of my brother in law's hair clients. Can you imagine the wisdom talks that can come from the great Tiger Woods?

Example moves the world more than doctrine.
-By Henry Miller

MARK
AQUIRRE

Seen here is <u>*Mark Aguirre*</u> and I. *He is an American former basketball player in the national Basketball Association. Aquirre was chosen as the first overall pick of the 1981 NBA draft by the Dallas Mavericks after playing three years at DePaul University.*

I ran into Mark during my husband's 35th anniversary celebration at McCormick Place. He is a big fan of Farley Jackmaster Funk's House Music style of DJing. Mark is also my Facebook friend which is kind of fascinating to see that someone so famous follows us and appreciates the work that we do in Chicago's communities.

Below is a photo of <u>*Stephen A. Smith*</u>. *He is an American sports television personality, sports radio host and sports journalist. Smith is a commentator on ESPN's First Take, where he appears with Max Kellerman and Molly Qerim. He also makes frequent appearances as an NBA analyst on Sports Center and works on the First Take Sports Talk Show.*

This photo was also taken at Steve Harvey's Neighborhood Awards in Las Vegas. I was in the same room with Mr. Smith, getting interviews for our grass-root Kidz Korna tv talk show as well. God was opening up some really great doors for me in this time and I didn't realize it much back then.

STEPHEN A. SMITH

This photo of **Andrena Hiltonen** (*my sister,
minister and prayer partner*) with the great <u>*Isiah Thomas*</u>. He is *an
American former professional basketball player, coach and executive who is an analyst for NBA on TNT. A point guard, the 12-time
NBA All-Star was named one of the 50 Greatest Players in NBA
History and inducted into the Naismith Memorial Basketball Hall
of Fame.*

My sister lives in Georgia but, came to Chicago for our annual
family reunion. Upon our weekend of fun and festivities, we went
to Father Pfleger's celebrity basketball game to help cure violence.
The games are always fun, safe and entertaining for the community.

Below is a photo of <u>*Jakeem Noah*</u>. *He is a French-American professional basketball player. He played college basketball for the Florida
Gators, winning back-to-back NCAA championships in 2006 and
2007. The Chicago Bulls selected Noah with the ninth overall pick
of the 2007 NBA draft.*

Noah was also a part of this celebrity basketball game to help prevent
violence. Many of Chicago residences looks forward to these yearly
events and a special thanks to every professional player that comes
out to support the cause for free and for mentorship opportunities
to assist underserved families.

<u>Jakeem Noah</u>.

From the errors of others, a wise man corrects his own.
-By Publilus Syrus

FORMER MAYOR DALEY

Seen here is the former *Mayor Richard Daley* and I.   *He's an American politician who served as the 54th Mayor of Chicago, Illinois from 1989 to 2011. Daley was elected mayor in 1989 and was re-elected five times until declining to run for a seventh term.*

Daley was the very first mayor to honor our work with a city of Chicago Proclamation letter on behalf of championing at-risk youth with our youth organization and local tv show. I couldn't believe that he found what I love doing, worthy of such an honor, but these where the small nuggets that kept us motivated to keep working.

Below is a photo of the *late former Mayor Eugene Sawyer* and I. *He was an American businessman, educator and politician. Sawyer was selected as the 53rd Mayor of Chicago, Illinois after the sudden death of then-mayor Harold Washington, serving from December 2, 1987 until April 24, 1989. Sawyer was the second African-American to serve as Mayor of Chicago.*

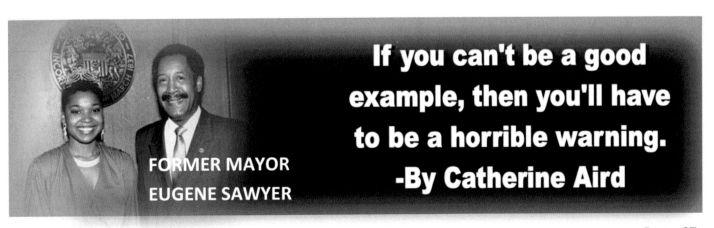

FORMER MAYOR EUGENE SAWYER

If you can't be a good example, then you'll have to be a horrible warning.
-By Catherine Aird

CAROL MOSELEY BRAUN

> There is a difference between imitating a good man and counterfeiting him.
> -By Benjamin Franklin

I had the opportunity to meet the former *Senator Carol Mosley Braun*. *She is an American diplomat, politician and lawyer who represented Illinois in the United States Senate from 1993 to 1999.*

This was also a photo moment from my Ms. Mahogany (beauty queen) days. Senator Braun stopped her work that day, just to pose for the camera with me. Again, this is another hindsight moment.   I can now think of how valuable, words of wisdom, mentoring and guidance from very important and successful people can be, if you will take the time to listen. Many of them have been, where you are trying to go.

Suzanna A. Mendoza is married to my childhood friend's cousin. *She's an American politician and 10th Comptroller of Illinois, serving since December 2016. A member of the Democratic Party, she formerly served as Chicago City Clerk and as an Illinois State Representative, representing the 1st District of Illinois.* My childhood friend's name is Robert Szostak from Iron Mountain Michigan and he wanted to make sure that I meet and glean from her wisdom since we both live in Chicago. Seen here is Suzanna, her husband and I.

> Nothing is so infectious as example.
> -By Francois de La Rochefolucauld

SUZANNA A. MENDOZA

**COMMISSIONER
STANLEY MOORE**

Everything change but change itself.
-By John F. Kennedy

Seen here is <u>*Commissioner Stanley Moore*</u> and I. *He's a member of the Cook County Board of Commissioners who has represented the 4th district since his appointment on April 11, 2013. The 4th district covers both Chicago and some surrounding Suburbs.*

On this day, I received a *Cook County Resolution Letter* on behalf of our community work. I am very grateful for Commissioner Moore for this honor. During this same ceremony, my husband was honored for his life-time contribution and co-creation of House Music. Below is the day that my husband also received a street sign in honor of his contribution to house music as well. Chance the Rapper's dad, <u>*Mr. Ken Bennett*</u> is seen here in front of the microphone. He was presenting Farley with a Proclamation Letter on behalf of the former **Mayor Rahm Emanuel**.

Mr. Bennett also offered to assist in every way that he can to help with the construction of the International House Music Museum and Hall of Fame as it is destined to be built here in Chicago.

KEN
BENNETT

Choices are hinges of destiny.
-By Edwin Markham

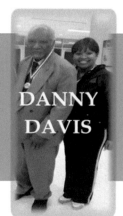

Life is just a series of trying to make up your mind. -By Timothy Fuller

DANNY DAVIS

Seen here is <u>*Congressman Danny Davis*</u> and I. *He's an American politician for U.S. Congress in Illinois for 1996. Davis resided in a block outside the 7th Congressional district, but he was familiar in the district.* This day, I was receiving an award from the Mahogany Heritage Foundation at Malcolm X College, again under the leadership of Mary Swopes. Each year, she honored movers and shakers from elders to young people whose making things happen amongst African Americans. The Honorable Congressman Davis is a great supporter of Mary's work, and he's always there to assist her whenever possible.

Below is a photo of the <u>*Alderman Pat Dowell*</u> and Farley. *Dowell was elected Alderman for the 3rd ward in 2007 and has been every since. She is a member of the City Council's Housing and Real Estate, Transportation and the Public Way, Landmarks, Rules and Health Committees.*

Alderman Dowell and the former **Alderman Bob Fioretti** are responsible for helping to get Farley's street sign up in the south loop area of down town Chicago. It's located on the same block where Farley was a resident DJ in a building called the Playground/Candy Store in the 80s.

ALD. PAT Dowell

If you want to make enemies, try and change something. -By Woodrow Wilson

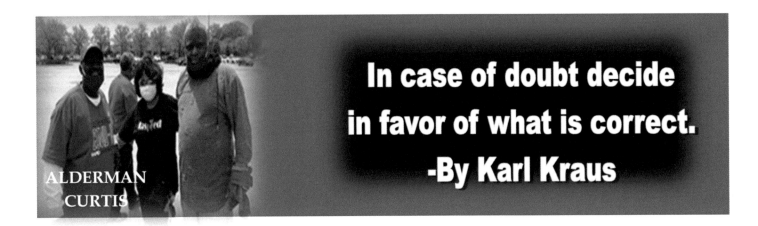

In case of doubt decide in favor of what is correct.
-By Karl Kraus

ALDERMAN CURTIS

Seen here is a photo moment of <u>**Alderman Derek Curtis**</u>, myself and my husband. *Curtis is an American politician who has served as the alderman of Chicago's 18th ward since 2015. He became the Democratic committee-man of the ward in 2011.* We are wearing our mask which means that this is a photo taken from the year of 2020. We were out in the community, helping to pass out thousands of food boxes to needy families for Covid relief. Upon your level of success, never forget to be a blessing to others. This is the one thing that my husband and I definitely have in common. We love being a blessing to others as God has blessed us to be.

Below is the beautiful <u>*Melissa Conyears-Ervin,*</u> *Chicago's City Treasurer in Illinois. Conyears-Ervin assumed office on May 20, 2019. She is a former Democratic member of the Illinois house of Representatives, representing District 10.* We took this photo in the sky box at the Soldier's Field football stadium which is home of the Chicago Bears. She's my Facebook friend and you can also catch her praying and doing live ministry shows, right on Facebook.

How dangerous can false reasoning prove.
-By Sophocles

MELISSA CONYEARS ERVIN

Pick battles big enough to matter, small enough to win.
-By Jonathan Kozel

ALD. CARRIE AUSTIN

Seen here is the <u>*Honorable Alderman Carrie Alston*</u> and I. *Carrie was Alderman of the 34th ward on Chicago's far south side. The predominantly African-American ward includes portions of Morgan Park and Roseland.* We were at her grand opening of Mansfield's shopping mall that she was able to bring into her ward. She invited me to be a vendor at the event to promote our youth program. We gave out school supplies that day and she was gracious enough to come and help pass them out too.

Below is a photo of <u>*Alderman David Moore and I.*</u> *He's another member of the Chicago City Council serving as Alderman for the 17th ward. This 2nd term Alderman is forecasted to be around for the city's progressive movement a long time.* Alderman Moore also does great work for his community. You can often catch him posting Facebook live feeds covering various projects that he does frequently and, he's a very hands on Alderman. In fact, they overwhelmingly voted him in for another term. He is also a great supporter of Kidz Korna.

ALD. DAVID MOORE

Many persons of high intelligence have notoriously poor judgement.
-By Sydney J. Harris

Seen here is a photo of the *Lieutenant Governor Juliana Stratton*. She holds the second highest executive office of the State of Illinois. *Stratton is an American lawyer and politician serving as the 48th lieutenant governor, since 2019. She previously served a Democratic member of the Illinois House of Representatives from 2017 to 2019.* I met her one night at a social outing. I always wanted a chance to tell her that we are proud of her for being a young sister representing a really great office and representing young black women well with what she does. Some weeks followed and with her help, my youth program received another honor, a letter of recognition from the Governor's office. This is a great honor for us and it makes our youth group proud.

ALD.
HOWARD
BROOKINS

Seen here is the honorable *Alderman Howard Brookins, elected as Alderman of the 21st ward in 2003, reelected in 2007, 2011, 2015 and 2019.* Brookins is also a great supporter our work. This is a photo of him speaking at one of our earlier events in 2007. He's also responsible for us having a street sign on 79th and Ashland in Chicago.

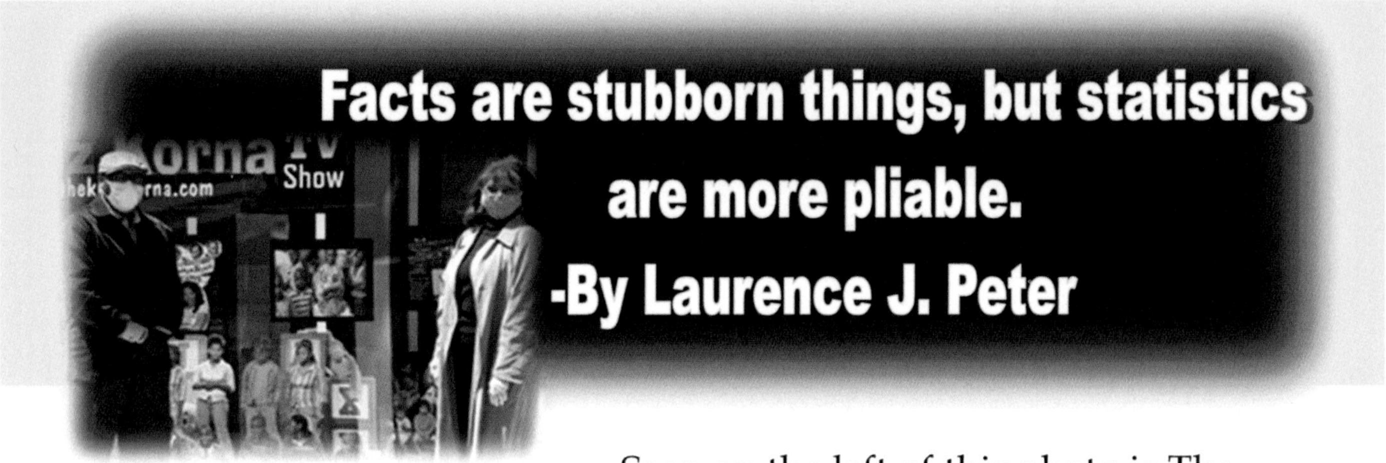

Facts are stubborn things, but statistics are more pliable.
-By Laurence J. Peter

Seen on the left of this photo is The *Mayor James Ford* of Country Club Hills. *He began his 1st term on May 1, 2015 as the first African American Mayor Elected. To the right is the House of Representative Debbie Meyers-Martin. She's a Democratic member of the Illinois House of Representatives for the 38th district. Meyers-Martin was also the Community Affairs Marketing Specialist for the Illinois State Treasurer's Office from April of 2007 until 2018.*

I had the privilege of working with both of them in regards to producing another charitable event for Covid Relief. We at Kidz Korna, had thousands of face mask, donated by Dr. Willie Wilson and we gave them away around the city including Country Club Hills. The Mayor and Meyers-Martin helped to distribute them that day.

Seen here is *Alderman Stephanie Coleman of 16th ward and Democratic Party Committeeman.* In this moment, we were out at a candle light vigil in support of some families whose relatives lost their lives to senseless gun violence in Chicago. Lord, Help Us!

Some persons are very decisive when it comes to avoiding decisions.
by Brendan Francis

ALD. STEPHANIE COLEMAN

If matters go badly now,
they will not always be so.
-By Horace

DONDA
WEST

Seen here is Kanye West's mom, the *late Dr. Donda West.* *She is former chairwoman of Chicago State University's English department.* She was such an inspiration to us in my earlier years of starting Kidz Korna. She endorsed the way that I spell the name. She also told me that it represents an urban appeal and a creative way that our young people can express themselves for change. Every since, we've been doing just that at Kidz Korna. The photo of her and I was taken at Chicago State University, one week, right before she passed away.

Below is a photo of the *late Heavy D* and I. *He is an Jamaican-born American rapper, record, singer and actor. He was the former leader of Heavy D & the Boyz, a group which included dancers and background vocalists. The group maintained a sizable audience in the United States through most of the 1990's.* This photo was taken at the Soul Train awards also on the night that notorious BIG was murdered. He was one of the celebrities that I had quick words with and he's no longer here either.

Delece with Heavy D

Pain is hard to bear, but with
patience, day by day, even
this shall pass away.
-By Theodore Tilton

MAYOR RUDY CLAY

Seen here is a blurry photo of the <u>*Late Gary Indiana Mayor Rudy Clay*</u> and I. *Rudolph Clay was an American Democratic politician. He served as the Mayor of Gary, Indiana and member of the Indiana Senate from 1972 to 1976.* This photo was taken at Michael Jackson's memorial when the city of Gary was honoring his legacy after he died. That year, I also met and interviewed **Fred Williamson,** (*professional actor and football player*) and others as thousands from around the world came out to celebrate Michael's legacy too.

The photo below was taken at the Chicago Urban League Conference at the McCormick Place. We were allowed to bring our youth group there for a learning and training experience amongst many great leaders. Seen here is the late <u>*Dr. Willie Barrows, an American civil rights activist and minister. Barrow was the co-founder of Operation PUSH, alongside Rev. Jesse Jackson*</u>. She is no longer here, but again what she did and who she was, like all of our great leaders, their stories deserves to be told. The person to the right is Shirley Richardson, my friend who is no longer with us as well. The value of true friendship is equally important. Her strength was my bridge while embarking on this journey. Your friends will be important to you along the way too.

WILLIE BARROWS

Without heroes we are all plain people, and don't know how far we can go.
-By Bernard Malamud

THANK YOU

Thanks for reading and/or exploring your legacy options as you too, can now **"Stand On the Shoulders of Giants."**

I never knew that one day, I would be writing a book simply by sharing my photo moments and giving inspiration to others through words of wisdom byway of QUOTES.

THANK YOU LORD FOR THIS DIVINELY INSPIRED IDEA.

Whatever you're doing, I hope you are thinking about or creating your legacy idea right now too, starting with these ***"Stars and Stirring Words"*** to help you along the way, and remember:

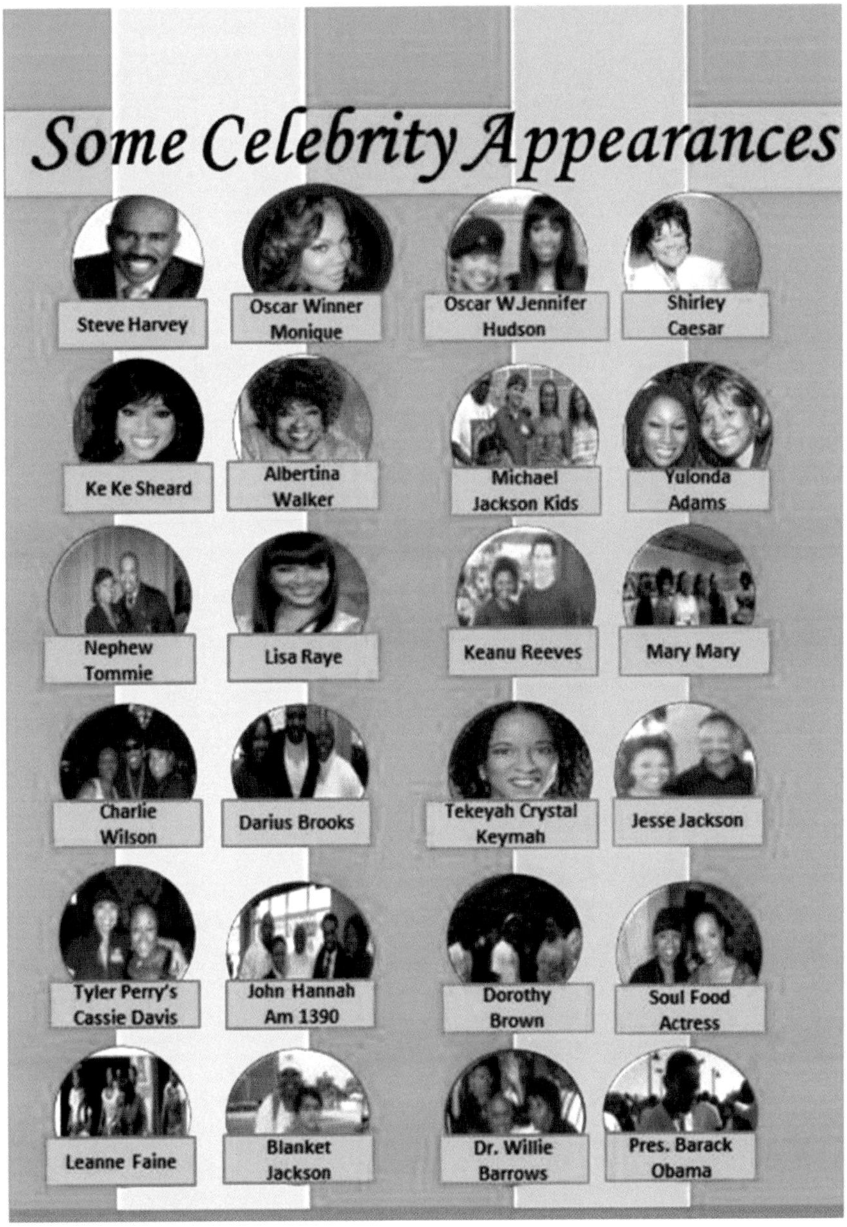

Some Celebrity Appearances
Steve Harvey
Oscar Winner Monique
Oscar W.Jennifer Hudson
Shirley Caesar
Ke Ke Sheard
Albertina Walker
Michael Jackson Kids
Yulonda Adams
Nephew Tommie
Lisa Raye
Keanu Reeves
Mary Mary
Charlie Wilson
Darius Brooks
Tekeyah Crystal Keymah
Jesse Jackson
Tyler Perry's Cassie Davis
John Hannah Am 1390
Dorothy Brown
Soul Food Actress
Leanne Faine
Blanket Jackson
Dr. Willie Barrows
Pres. Barack Obama

Philippians 4:13

"You can do all things with Christ that Strengthens You," according to God's word (this quote is taken from the Bible, in Philippians, Chapter 4 verse 13).

Our minds can shape the way a thing will be because we act according to our expectations. -By Federico Fellini

on the Kidz Korna Tv Show

Tyler Perry

Fantasia

Tramaine Hawkins

Judge Mathis

Holly Roinson Pete

Katherine Jackson

Anthony Hamilton

Former Mayor Daley

Rushion McDonald

Tye Tribbet

Paris Jackson

U & Me Morning Show

BET's Ed Gorden

Kim Whitley

Musiq soul Child

Tyler Perry's Daddy Girl

Les Brown

BET Past Owner Bob Johnson

Donda West

Donnie McClurkin

Joe Jackson

Earvin Johnson

Tyler Perry's LaVan Davis

Cory the Comedian

BOOK DISCLAIMER

This book is written for the purpose of news and information on behalf of the Kidz Korna Tv Show. It's also a tool to guide conversations between multi-generational communication barriers and it encourages inspirational productivity.

You must have the right view of you, so that your life can move in the right direction. We must see, what we want to be, and I have just shown you so much greatness through these photos.

Also, each celebrity's mini bio sample is taken from Wikipedia, to show you a measure of value as to what goals you can aim for.

Now, Lets aim to go higher together and don't forget to Clap for all of your personal victories too.

Willie Perry Jr. as DJ Casper

In this moment, I'm also reminded of the song "Clap, Clap, Clap Your Hands." These words are taken from the *late Casper of the Cha Cha Slide*. As I am finishing this book, my husband and I are working with the family to prepare his funeral. **Please do all that you can to value your life and the gifts that God gave you!** RIP our personal friend! *His song is one of the most famous re-occurring songs of all time, coming from Chicago.*

BEFORE YOU CLOSE THIS BOOK,

Please understand the importance of communication.

Beyond my wildest dreams, I'd never thought that I'd one day visit the White House and later to become a certified agent, (*given authority to bestow honor to others*) that represents the highest office of the land.

After becoming a recipient of the **Prestigious Presidential Lifetime Achievement Award for my volunteerism service** signed by the current President, I now get to honor others in the United States of America. It's all because I decided to keep listening, keep communicating, keep praying and to keep moving in spite of.

Upon discovering that **doing is being**, it made me realize that after hanging around all of these stars, important people, dignitaries and etc., I may not be as powerful as some, but what I was doing is being the best me that I can be and someone very powerful noticed.

My help comes:

♦ *Through **Communication** and the **Wisdom of Elders**,*

♦ *Having **Tunnel Vision** from the pain of my **Ancestors** to keep PUSHing (**P**ray **U**ntil **S**omething **H**appens) through,* and

♦ *Lastly, from being in tuned with **GOD** 's grace for* **Spiritual Guidance**, **Instruction** *and* **Strength** *to create my own lane for victorious living* and you can have victorious living too.

Other Projects

*CIF Ministry Productions

*Queens Awards Ceremony

cifproduction.com
queenrewarded.com

For more *Stars and Stirring Words*: Volume 2 — **On The Shoulders of Giants** (*Youth Edition*) and Volume 3 — **On The Shoulders of Angels** (*Inspirational*), are available. Go to **www.drdelece.com | drdelece@hotmail.com**

Dr. Delece's Back Story for producing this book.

The goal was to help guide you through some battlefields of your life using words of wisdom. Did you know that there is POWER in what you say to yourself. In the Bible (Proverbs 18:21), it tells us that Life and Death is in the power of your tongue? What you say, makes a great deal of differences with your circumstances and just know that GOD WILL BACK YOU UP, if you allow it be so.

This **STAR STUDDED** Inspirational montage of quotes has wisdom notes for every *GENERATION AND MANY SITUATIONS* collaged on each page as I talked about my journey for success.

Dr. Delece
Williams

I WENT BACK TO GO FORWARD

At around sixteenish, my siblings and I had a pet <u>CALF</u>.

Most girls grow up with a puppy, hamster, bird or even a garden snake for a pet. There I was sitting with a calf, not realizing the significance of this photo until now. Yes, it was definitely impossible at that time to understand it for sure.

It has also indulged me with memories of my sweet sixteenish years, recalling the excitement in life as I began searching for bigger and better adventures to aim for beyond family concerns, classmates connections and school activities.

Life was actually going to soon happen without living at home and I needed to figure out how to turn my dreams into reality, what direction to take, what moves to make or was I going to find all the answers by going to College.

In case you are thinking, why are you talking about a cow in this moment, glad you asked! That cow represented the <u>maturity</u> (**HAVING REACHED FULL DEVELOPMENT**) of which most 16 year olds definitely don't know much about. It usually comes as you get older, and that I surely needed it in my next phase of life.

No one knows a clear path of discovering yourself, your mission and/or your future while looking through the eyes of your youth, like the young me on the other page, to becoming the blossoming adult that I was aspiring to be on this page. Hindsight is definitely 20/20 and we most certainly don't have a measuring stick of solutions to help make goals obtainable unless you have experiences from others, our instincts, wit and knowledge to help you along the way.

I remember wearing this dress to the Naacp Image Awards in the early 90's during my reign as Ms. Mahogany, a beauty pageant winner. Upon meeting many celebrities backstage, my shoe heel broke. It was a gentleman from a fancy store in Hollywood California that gave me a pair of $300 dollar shoes for free and told me to always remember to help someone else along the way. He had also spoke into my spirit that led me to believe that I could be someone great one day.

It has always been words of wisdom that stuck with me while navigating my goals from working in television, producing, writing, to modeling and helping to shape young bright minds for **over 30** years, along with marrying a world famous Music Producer/DJ and friend of over **38 years**. Words of wisdom has always help to sharpen my intuition, giving me light at the end of the tunnel thus creating a pathway for my ends to meet. Thanks God for victorious living today and the strength to help others along the way. Hope this was helpful!

AuthorHouse™
1663 Liberty Drive
Bloomington, IN 47403
www.authorhouse.com
Phone: 833-262-8899

Because of the dynamic nature of the Internet, any web addresses or links contained in this book may have changed
since publication and may no longer be valid. The views expressed in this work are solely those of the author and do
not necessarily reflect the views of the publisher, and the publisher hereby disclaims any responsibility for them.

Any people depicted in stock imagery provided by Getty Images are models,
and such images are being used for illustrative purposes only.
Certain stock imagery © Getty Images.

This book is printed on acid-free paper.

Scripture quotations marked KJV are from the Holy Bible, King James Version (Authorized Version). First published
in 1611. Quoted from the KJV Classic Reference Bible, Copyright © 1983 by The Zondervan Corporation.

ISBN: 979-8-8230-0618-7 (sc)
ISBN: 979-8-8230-0619-4 (e)

Print information available on the last page.

Published by AuthorHouse 09/04/2024

authorHOUSE

Printed in the United States
by Baker & Taylor Publisher Services